W9-ATY-454

Astronauts Working in Space

CAPSTONE PRESS
a capstone imprint

Angela Royston

First Facts is published by Capstone Press, a Capstone imprint,
151 Good Counsel Drive, P.O. Box 669, Mankato, Minnesota 56002.
www.capstonepub.com

First published in 2010 by A&C Black Publishers Limited, 36 Soho Square, London W1D 3QY
www.acblack.com
Copyright © A&C Black Ltd. 2010

Produced for A&C Black by Calcium. www.calciumcreative.co.uk

032010
005746ACF10

Library of Congress Cataloging-in-Publication Data
Royston, Angela, 1945-
  Astronauts working in space / by Angela Royston.
    p. cm. — (First facts, big picture)
  Includes index.
  ISBN 978-1-4296-5512-5 (library binding)
  ISBN 978-1-4296-5522-4 (paperback)
  1. Astronautics—Juvenile literature. I. Title. II. Series.
TL793.R6185 2011
629.45—dc22   2010011207

Every effort has been made to trace copyright holders and to obtain their permission for use of copyright material.

This book is produced using paper that is made from wood grown in managed, sustainable forests. It is natural,
renewable and recyclable. The logging and manufacturing processes conform to the environmental regulations
of the country of origin.

Acknowledgements

The publishers would like to thank the following for their kind permission to reproduce their photographs:

Cover: Shutterstock: Tischenko Irina (front), Alle (back). **Pages:** NASA: 4-5, 10-11, 20, Goddard Space Flight
Center 6, Human Space Flight Collection 1, 9, 12-13, 14-15, 19, 21, 24, Johnson Space Center 3, 16-17, Marshall
Space Flight Center 5; Shutterstock: Devation/Edwin Verbruggen 18-19, Dr_Flash 18, Eric G 8, Jean-Luc 14-15
(background), William Attard McCarthy 6-7 (background), Remy Bejear Merriex 8-9, Shukaylov Roman 20-21,
Skobrik 10, Snaprender 2-3, 7, Ekaterina Starshaya 22-23, Taily 10-11 (background), 12-13 (background), Vicente
Barcelo Varona 16-17 (background), WilleeCole 12

Contents

Blast Off!

A **spacecraft** is on the launchpad. Inside are five **astronauts**, waiting to blast into **space**.

Into the air

The **rockets** start up. Engines roar and the spacecraft lifts into the air.

5, 4, 3, 2, 1

Rocket power

A huge tank is filled with **fuel** for the spacecraft's engines. When the fuel is used up, the tank and **booster** rockets fall off, and back to Earth.

Two booster rockets help to power the spacecraft into the sky.

5

Into Space

Astronauts in space can see the Earth far below them. They can see blue oceans and white clouds.

Around and around

The spacecraft travels very fast. It **orbits** Earth. This means that it goes round and round Earth.

A spacecraft takes one and a half hours to orbit Earth.

Starlight

The spacecraft flies from light to dark as it orbits Earth. When it is dark, the astronauts see billions of bright stars.

Floating

The astronauts float inside the spacecraft. They push themselves off the walls to move around.

Stick it down!

Everything floats in space. Astronauts stick things to **Velcro** patches on the spacecraft walls to stop them from floating away.

Wheeee!

No gravity

On Earth, a **force** called gravity pulls you down to the ground. There is no gravity in space so everything floats!

Floating in space is easier than swimming in water!

9

Dinnertime

The food astronauts eat is cooked on Earth before they leave. It is then packed into the spacecraft.

Drink up

Astronauts drink through straws from containers. If they used a cup, all the liquid would float away in tiny drops!

Snack attack

Floating food

Astronauts heat food in the spacecraft oven. They have to eat it very carefully—if they move the spoon too fast it will float away!

It's not easy to eat in space!

Bathtime

Astronauts have a special shower in the spacecraft. They cannot just turn on the faucet to get water!

No splashes in space!

Astronauts wash with a damp sponge. They use special shampoo to wash their hair. It does not need to be rinsed out.

Scrub-a-dub!

Drying off

Astronauts use a machine like a small vacuum cleaner, which sucks all the water off their bodies.

We still use towels to dry our hair!

Hold on Tight

The astronauts' sleeping bags are fixed to the wall. This stops them from floating while they are asleep!

Sleep well

Straps hold the astronaut onto the bed and help them to lie flat.

Zzzzzz

Astronauts still dream in space.

Toilets too!

An astronaut even has to strap himself to the toilet. Air sucks away everything in the toilet so it can't escape!

Spacewalk

Sometimes astronauts have to work outside the spacecraft. Then they wear a **spacesuit**.

Staying alive

The spacesuit gives air and everything else the astronaut needs to stay alive.

Astronauts are tied to the spacecraft so they do not float away.

Helmet

Space danger

There is no air to breathe in space. Without a spacesuit, the astronaut would die. The spacesuit also stops the astronaut from getting too hot or cold.

Gloves

Hello Earth!

The astronauts are alone in space, but they can talk to people back on Earth.

In control

From space, the astronauts talk to Mission Control. This is a group of people on Earth who control the space mission.

See you soon!

Hi there!

Astronauts can be in space for many months. They write **e-mails** to their families back on Earth. Sometimes, they can talk to their families by telephone.

Even in space, e-mails can be sent!

Back to Earth

To return to Earth, the astronauts slow the spacecraft down. Then it falls toward the Earth.

Time to land

As it nears the Earth, the spacecraft slows down and glides to the ground.

We're back!

Wobbly legs

It takes several days for the astronauts to get used to being back on Earth. Floating makes their muscles weak. They have to exercise to make them strong again.

The astronauts tell everyone about their space trip.

Glossary

astronauts people who travel into space

booster something that gives extra power

e-mails letters sent from one computer to another

force a push or a pull that changes the way something moves

fuel something that is burned to give heat or make an engine work

orbits travels in a path around something in space

rockets powerful engines that burn fuel very fast

space everything in the universe

spacecraft a vehicle that travels into space

spacesuit special clothes that allow an astronaut to survive in space outside the spacecraft

Velcro furry material that things can be stuck on to

Further Reading

FactHound offers a safe, fun way to find Internet sites related to this book. All of the sites on FactHound have been researched by our staff.

Here's all you do:

Visit www.facthound.com

FactHound will fetch the best sites for you!

Books

Astronauts (Graphic Careers) by David West, Franklin Watts (2008).

Astronaut Handbook by Meghan McCarthy, Alfred A. Knopf (2008).

Space (Extreme Survival) by Angela Royston, Rigby (2004).

Index